AF089069

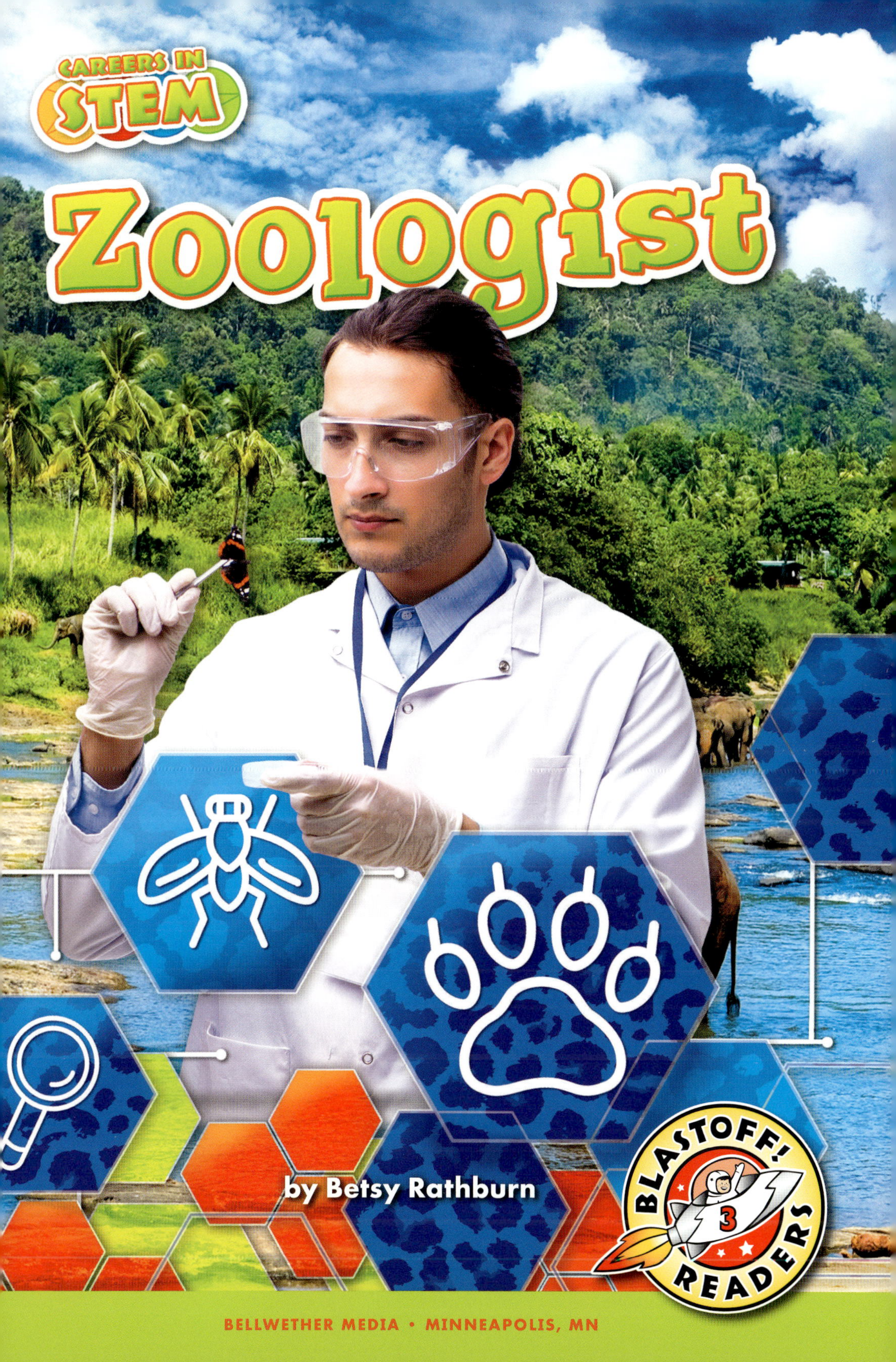
CAREERS IN
STEM
Zoologist
by Betsy Rathburn
BLASTOFF!
3
READERS
BELLWETHER MEDIA • MINNEAPOLIS, MN

Blastoff! Readers are carefully developed by literacy experts to build reading stamina and move students toward fluency by combining standards-based content with developmentally appropriate text.

Level 1 provides the most support through repetition of high-frequency words, light text, predictable sentence patterns, and strong visual support.

Level 2 offers early readers a bit more challenge through varied sentences, increased text load, and text-supportive special features.

Level 3 advances early-fluent readers toward fluency through increased text load, less reliance on photos, advancing concepts, longer sentences, and more complex special features.

★ **Blastoff! Universe**

Reading Level

Grade K

Grades 1–3

Grade 4

This edition first published in 2023 by Bellwether Media, Inc.

Library of Congress Cataloging-in-Publication Data

Names: Rathburn, Betsy, author.
Title: Zoologist / by Betsy Rathburn.
Description: Minneapolis, MN : Bellwether Media, Inc., 2023. | Series: Blastoff! Readers: Careers in STEM | Includes bibliographical references and index. | Audience: Ages 5-8 | Audience: Grades 2-3 | Summary: "Simple text and full-color photography introduce beginning readers to zoologists. Developed by literacy experts for students in kindergarten through third grade"–Provided by publisher.
Identifiers: LCCN 2022036387 (print) | LCCN 2022036388 (ebook) | ISBN 9798886871395 (library binding) | ISBN 9798886872651 (ebook)
Subjects: LCSH: Zoologists–Juvenile literature.
Classification: LCC QL50.5 .R38 2023 (print) | LCC QL50.5 (ebook) | DDC 590.92–dc23/eng/20220819
LC record available at https://lccn.loc.gov/2022036387
LC ebook record available at https://lccn.loc.gov/2022036388

Editor: Elizabeth Neuenfeldt Designer: Andrea Schneider

Printed in the United States of America, North Mankato, MN.

Table of Contents

Watching Elephants

A zoologist studies animals from afar. She spots a family of elephants. She watches them find food and water. She studies how they get along.

Her work helps people understand elephants and other animals!

What Is a Zoologist?

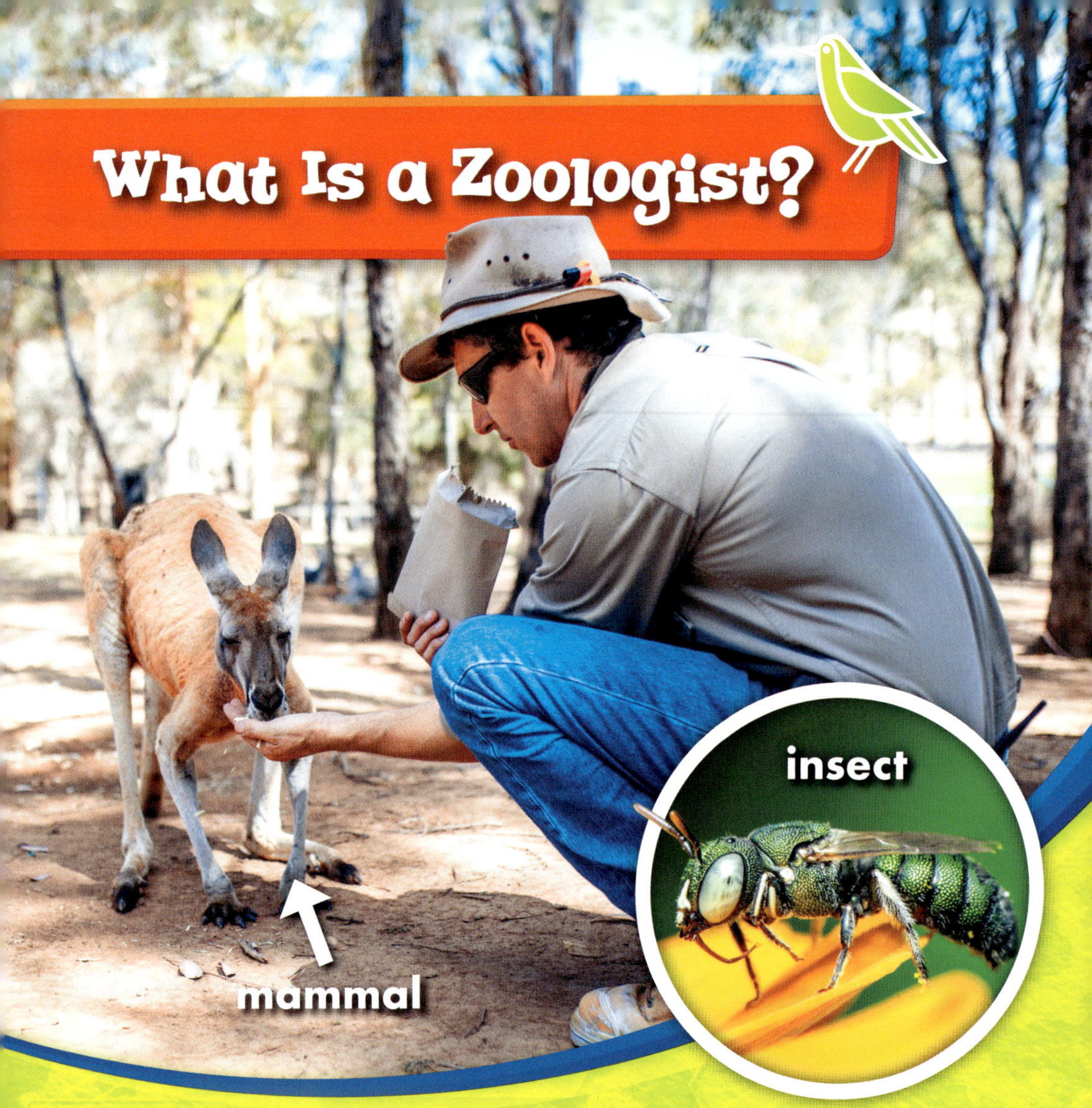

Zoologists are scientists. They study animals. Many study **mammals** or birds. Others study fish or **insects**. Some learn about **reptiles**.

They study how animals live. They find different ways to keep animals safe.

Famous Zoologist
Name
Katy Payne
Born
1937
Birthplace
Ithaca, New York
Schooling
Cornell University
Known For
Studied how humpback whales and elephants use sounds to talk

Many zoologists work outside. They study animals in their **habitats** or in zoos.

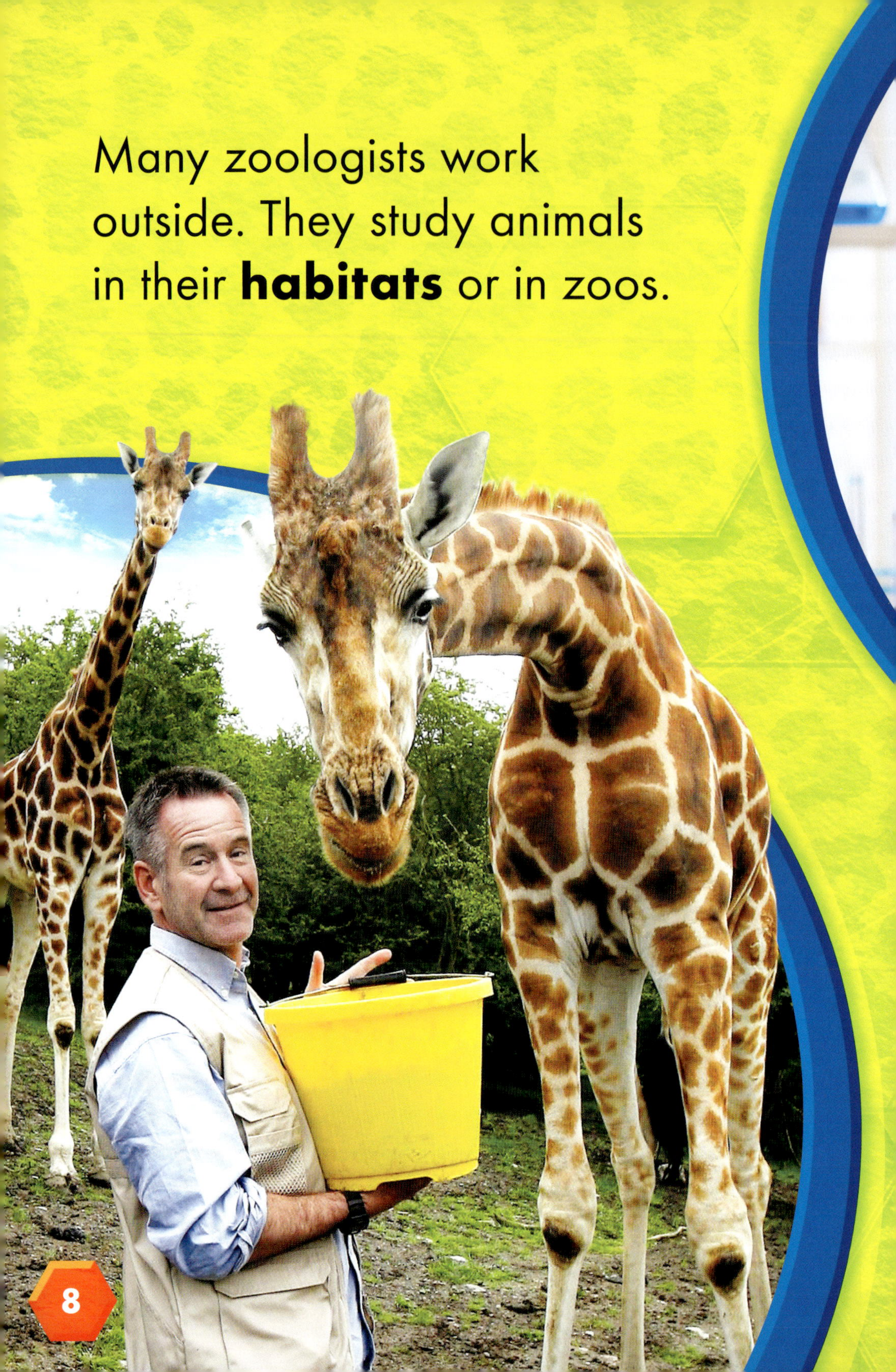

Some zoologists do **research** in offices. They work in **labs**, too. Some teach students about animals in classrooms.

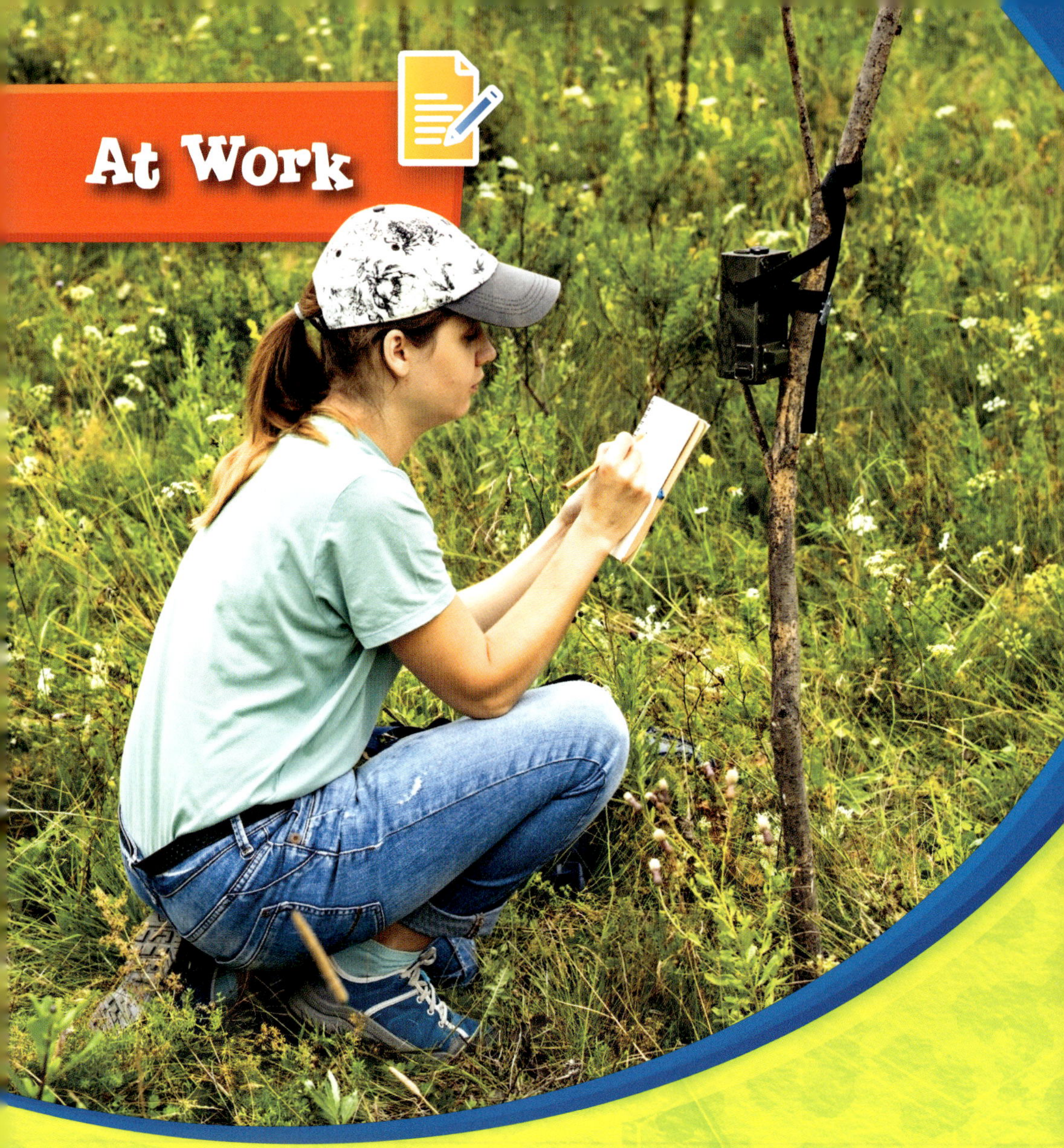

Zoologists study animal **behavior**. They watch animals from a distance. They learn how animals hunt, eat, and find homes.

They write down what they find. This helps people understand how different animals live.

Zoology in Real Life

understand animals

keep animals in zoos healthy

keep animals safe

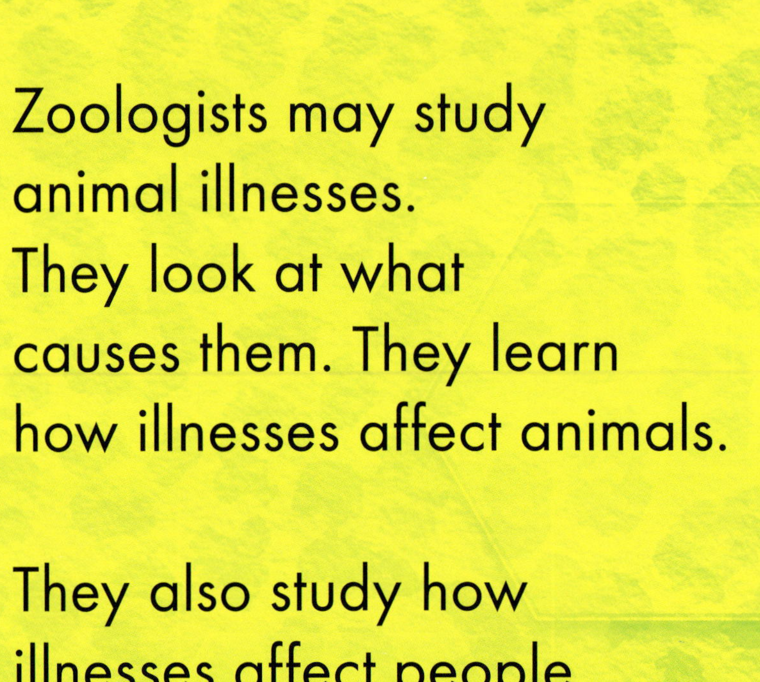

Zoologists may study animal illnesses. They look at what causes them. They learn how illnesses affect animals.

They also study how illnesses affect people and other animals. They work to keep animals and people safe.

Zoologists may study how **climate change** affects animals. They watch how it changes animal populations.

Using STEM

use biology to understand animals

Technology — use GPS tools to follow animals

create tools to help study animals

Math — study graphs and charts to follow animal populations

They follow animal populations with **GPS**. They create and study graphs. These help them see how much populations change.

Other zoologists study **endangered** animals. They try to understand why the animals are at risk.

They may try to keep animals safe. They save habitats from **invasive species**!

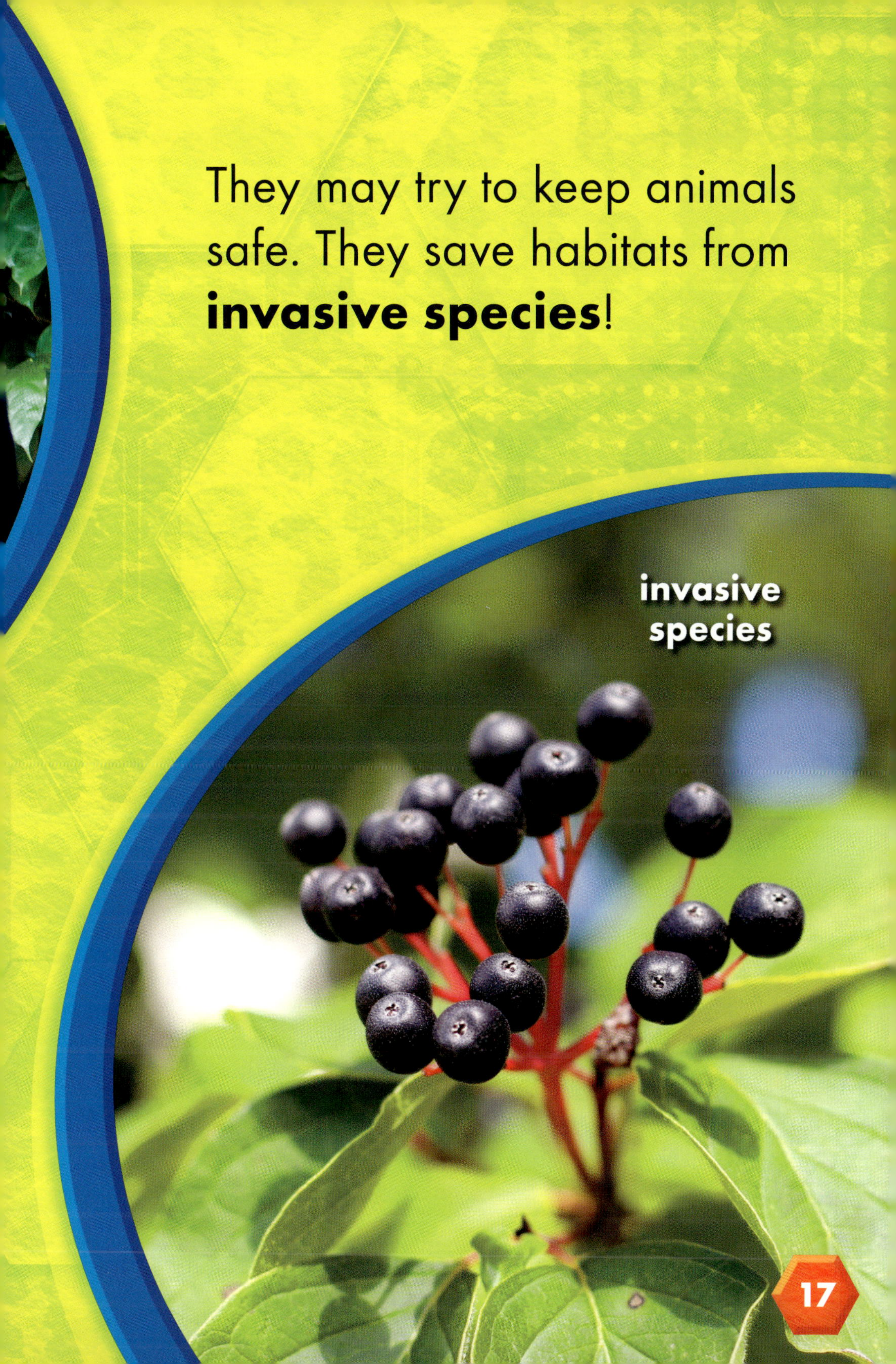

Becoming a Zoologist

Zoologists go to college. Many study **biology** or other sciences. They also study math.

After college, many keep learning. They go to **graduate school** to study a subject further.

biology
student

Some zoologists get a **doctorate**. They may work in colleges. They can lead research.

How to Become a Zoologist

1. study biology and other sciences in college
2. go to graduate school
3. find a job

Others find jobs right away. Their work helps people understand animals!

Glossary

behavior—the way that someone or something acts

biology—a science that deals with things that are alive

climate change—a human-caused change in Earth's weather due to warming temperatures

doctorate—the highest degree at a college; a doctorate is also called a PhD.

endangered—in danger of dying out

GPS—global positioning system; GPS is a system that uses satellites to find locations on Earth.

graduate school—a school where people study a specialty area after college

habitats—lands with certain types of plants, animals, and weather

insects—small animals with six legs and hard outer bodies; an insect's body is divided into three parts.

invasive species—a species that is not originally from a region that causes harm to its new region

labs—buildings with special tools to do science experiments and tests

mammals—warm-blooded animals that have backbones and feed their young milk

reptiles—cold-blooded animals that have backbones and lay eggs

research—careful study to find new knowledge or information about something

To Learn More

AT THE LIBRARY

Grack, Rachel. *Elephants*. Minneapolis, Minn.: Bellwether Media, 2022.

Herman, Gail. *What Is Climate Change?* New York, N.Y.: Penguin Workshop, 2018.

Moon, Derek. *Great Careers Working with Animals*. Lake Elmo, Minn.: Focus Readers, 2022.

ON THE WEB

FACTSURFER

Factsurfer.com gives you a safe, fun way to find more information.

1. Go to www.factsurfer.com.
2. Enter "zoologist" into the search box and click .
3. Select your book cover to see a list of related content.

Index

The images in this book are reproduced through the courtesy of: Elnur, front cover (zoologist), pp. 8-9; Valeriia Naumenko, front cover (background); Dirk Ercken, p. 3; Robert Styppa, p. 4; soft_light, pp. 4-5 (binoculars); AzmanL, pp. 6-7 (mammals); yod67 p. 6 (insect); Wiki Commons/ Wiki Commons, p. 7 (Katy Payne); PA Images/ Alamy, p. 8; B Christopher/ Alamy, p. 9 (teaching students); Lena_viridis, pp. 10-11; Adam Seward/ Alamy, p. 11 (understand animals); Gav Smith, p. 11 (keep animals in zoos healthy); Mia2you, p. 11 (keep animals safe); bari paramarta, p. 12; ShotPrime Studio, pp. 12-13; Design Pics Inc/ Alamy, pp. 14-15; Hemis/ Alamy, p. 15 (animal movement graph); Danny Ye, pp. 16-17; Nelly B, p. 17; Xinhua/ Alamy, p. 18; Jason Doucette/ Alamy, pp. 18-19 (biology student); Christian Kober 1/ Alamy, p. 20 (zoologist); Nature Picture Library/ Alamy, pp. 20-21 (seabird researcher); Rosa Jay, p. 23.